Influence Vs. Illusion

By: Logan Cader

Copyright © Logan Carder

Hardcover ISBN: 978-1-959820-66-6

Paperback ISBN: 978-1-959820-65-9

E-book ISBN: 978-1-959820-64-2

All rights reserved. No part of this publication may be reproduced, stored in a retrieval system, or transmitted in any form or by any means, electronic, mechanical, recording, or otherwise, without the prior written permission of the author.

Published by Author Ghost Writer. Buffalo Groove, Illinois.

Printed on acid-free paper.

Author Ghost Writer.

2023

Authorghostwriter.com

Table of Contents

Chapter 1 1

    Dawn of a Digital Metropolis 1

Chapter 2 14

    Footsteps of Yesterday: A Journey from Ambition to Achievement14

Chapter 3 29

    Echoes of Simplicity: Nostalgia in Hometown Harmony 29

Chapter 4 44

    Echoes of Progress: The Dance of Tradition and Innovation 44

Chapter 5 55

    Navigating the Digital Divide: Evolution of Talent Acquisition .. 55

Chapter 6 68

    Virtual Realities: The Allure and Peril of Digital Escapism.......... 68

Chapter 7 78

    Pixels and Paradoxes: Navigating the Social Media Landscape .. 78

Chapter 8 90

    Guardians of the Digital Realm: A Tale of Cybersecurity 90

Chapter 9 103

    Dancing with Doubt: Navigating the Affair with AI.................... 103

Chapter 10 111

    Finding Balance: Navigating the Digital and Real Worlds.......... 111

Chapter 1

Dawn of a Digital Metropolis

As I stepped out of my car and marveled at the cityscape before me—whispers of technology blocked my vision—augmented reality of the digital and physical. Innovation has transformed every area of life, and it's time for me to adapt and make sense of this new, brave world. The towering skyscrapers with the LEDs illuminated the night with a number of colors. It was 3:00 am, to be exact, and the streets were silent. No cacophony of horns, alarms, and engines. But there was an unusual feeling, a feeling that had come to define this new world. With every heartbeat, a pulse of progress surged through my veins, and it all seemed like a dream rendered in glass.

As I stepped into my apartment's building, I couldn't help but notice the advanced infrastructure. "I have never felt like this before; why is there a sudden shift of energy?" I questioned myself. The technological advancement of the building groped me instantly. The lobby was a symphony of high-quality materials. A whole new world propelled by innovation. The OLED panels shifted with the time of day, producing an ever-changing glow.

"How can elevators be so advanced?" Suddenly, I started noticing every minute detail. How come I have never given a thought about it before? The elevators, the futuristic contraptions, their LED touchscreens, I don't even have to select my destination; the face recognition at the entrance of the elevators makes a seamless transition. The elevators made a shift, a far cry from the creaky old elevators. The glass doors sealed shut as I entered the elevator, and I was enclosed in a transparent capsule. A blur of shimmering lights, angular architecture, everything felt different. The sensors even tracked my biometrics, and the temperature was adjusted to my liking. I feel unusual, or maybe I was thinking about the erratic jerks of the elevators that I left in town.

∙ ∙ ∙ ∙ ∙ ∙ ∙

As I reached my floor, the door opened. I stepped into a corridor that was an epitome of elegance and luxury. The walls were filled with art displays that changed with the rhythms of the city. The digital concierge hologram offered a warm entrance; my apartment was a high-tech wonderland. My apartment's door is also equipped with my face recognition; as the door opened—I was greeted by a minimalistic and inviting environment. The feel of my house is technologically integrated with how my emotions are. It feels extremely unreal at times, the technological advancement in the surroundings. I entered, and the lights dimmed, adjusting to my presence. The apartment was not just a place to live; it was a structure of the technological revolution. It was a reflection of the brave new world, a world where innovation and advancements meet.

• • • • • •

Thoughts took over my sleep, or maybe I was beyond exhausted. The long-haul flight had taken me on a journey that was not just connected with the physical miles but the boundaries of existence as well. It was more than the time zones, moving across the ocean and into the heart of a city that seemed to breathe on the pulses and rhythms of technology. My steps were heavier, and I was thinking about every inch of my apartment. I could feel the exhaustion and heaviness seeping into my soul. The stark, contrasting lights whispered a tale of transformation, a brave new world; where the surface of the society had been touched by the hands of innovation.

Yes, I was surrounded by digitalization!

• • • • • • •

Deep down, I craved silence. The simplicity of my bed, a safe haven—a sanctuary where I could treat myself countless times. A place where I could immerse myself in the depths of my thoughts, where the environment does not change with how I feel. My present home and bed was nothing but luxurious; the inviting embrace of my bed and the crisp linens cradled me into their softness. I couldn't help but wonder how technology while promising progress and convenience, was simultaneously taking away from the very essence of what it means to be human. It was as if the more advanced our technology became, the more we disconnected from the core of our humanity, the simple joys of face-to-face conversations, the profound depth of genuine creativity, and the unfiltered authenticity of our true selves.

But peace was nowhere to be found! As I changed my side, I couldn't stop myself from thinking about my journey. A reminder of my resilience. A reminder of whirlwind technology, the human touch still held sway.

• • • • • • •

The bedroom….my bedroom was no less than an oasis of serenity as the view was the heart of this world. The glass walls and the space provided panoramic views of the city. The towering skyscrapers and the streets were the walls of my inner sanctum, a constant reminder of how things have changed. The glow of the city's neon embrace, I could see the metropolis stretching. The massive towers and the futuristic buildings, the shimmering lights of digital dreams. The entire landscape was a work of art, a fusion of form and function. A place where design meets technology and dances rhythmically. Each building was an epitome of creativity of humanity. Each piece weaved with the possibilities of technology. The glass walls, from top to bottom, framed the entire landscape in a living, breathing painting. I felt like I could touch the neon glow with my hand as if the innovations coursed through the city's veins.

• • • • • • •

Influence vs Illusion

As I lay on the bed and my eyes fixed on the ceiling, I felt a sense of ambiguity. The transformation was not just limited to structures; it had gone through every essence of life. The streets were alive with electric vehicles, and the air seemed to whisper with the promises of progress. In this room, I felt stillness, a place of duality—a pace of technological advancement met with a sense of solace. The stunning views, minimalist design, overwhelming view of the city, and depth of my thoughts were a transformation of the cityscape. Everything was a testament of my transformation; the glass walls symbolized transparency. The lights of the city felt like a painted canvas of the night. I pondered over my struggles and held the key to my journey of self-discovery in this innovation-led reality. With my eyes closed, I surrendered to my exhaustion, allowing the bed to take the weight of my thoughts.

· · · · · · ·

In this moment of surrender, my mind took a flight. The city has evolved; it has been transformed by technology, and I evolved with it. In this new world, seeking to navigate technology, authenticity, and purpose. I reflected on the transformation; it was not just a place to rest. It was a contemplation in the heart of the new world. Maybe the existence had been redefined, or I was determined to uncover the truths that lay at its core.

· · · · · · ·

I arrived in this bustling city at a young age with dreams and aspirations. I was at the cusp of adulthood, eager to find a place, anxious to carve my niche in a world where technology had not only advanced but redefined. The city stretched out way before me, like a canvas painted with possibilities, and I was indeed determined to leave my mark. This book is my attempt to pen down the chronicles of my journey in this transformed reality the lessons I have learned, and to explore the challenges and opportunities that lie ahead. The world I once knew has evolved beyond my expectations. Hence, it is the time for me and for everyone to adapt and make sense of this new world. But here I will be dead honest with my thoughts and the power of being your true self and what impact looks like on others.

I decided to struggle to achieve my goals, and in those early days, I rented an apartment, nothing fancy, but I had a place to call my own, a place where I could sit and think; nonetheless, it was my humble abode. The space offered me solace during my dark times. I will never forget the shadows of my past.

In the early days, when I had first set foot in this city, brimming with dreams but down with uncertainties. I had no idea of the cold reality of the world and the challenges awaiting. My rented space was a reminder of my beginnings, a small enclave, the weathered walls and the creaking floors, a dark history. I had come to this city with dreams as big as the skyscrapers; the struggle was real, but I was not immune to them. I sent out job applications, a drop in the ocean of qualified professionals. Days turned into weeks and weeks into months. I was encircled round and round in the pool of interview rejections and was uncertain.

• • • • • • •

I remember vividly an interview experience that dented my confidence. Having optimism with me, when I entered the room, I came to know that only my experience and qualifications were going to be evaluated. The burden of judgment weighed heavily in the air, suffocating any expectation I had held on.

The questions that bombarded me seemed to compose my career history, every question an investigation into my previous attachments and credentials. It seemed like my very being was more than just dialogue; I felt I was turned into a curriculum vitae and a bullet point list. The judgment was more extensive than being able to demonstrate the skills and knowledge that I had.

In that instant, the stark reality dawned upon me: my potential was being evaluated via the pinhole of the past, and any variation or gap was judged with suspicion. What I had learned about my personality traits, my growth potential, and the lessons I had taken from my failures were almost oppressed.

Getting out of that interview room, my confidence was destroyed. It was more than just the issue of being judged by the merit; it felt like denial of the capacity for development and adaptation. The memory stuck, a recurring proof of the trials one has to grapple with to prove that one is more than mere credentials.

On the contrary, after a dissatisfying meeting, I made up my mind and started afresh with a never-ending strength in my heart. I took hold of the realization that the value I have does not merely encompass a resume; most times, the experiences were both effective and challenging.

· · · · · · ·

Now that I have everything, when I look back in the past, I was constantly rejected. The digital world was a mess, and there was no such thing as social media platforms or AI-driven algorithms to provide an escape from the realities of job search. I used to scroll carefully through the profiles, witnessing a world that seemed far from my own. It was not a filtered, perfected world, and not every moment was a snapshot of bliss. Every individual had flaws, and they worked hard to work on them.

• • • • • • •

Chapter 2

Footsteps of Yesterday: A Journey from Ambition to Achievement

Allow me to take you back—back to the moments that now reside in the rooms of memories. They are all clear to me, as it is a story of yesterday. In the quietude of my room, I often find myself getting back to the footsteps of a younger version of me.

I had a vision, a goal, an ambition—I wanted to climb the ladder and I was not afraid of the struggles. Coming from a family with no support, I was well aware and prepared for a difficult journey. I started with a job at a restaurant. It was not easy to get this job, but I left no stone unturned in proving myself as a good resource. My dreams were as grand as the skyscrapers covering the city's skyline. The struggles and the long hours were like the colors of my painting.

As I lay comfortably on my bed and close my eyes, I can feel myself traveling through the currents of time. The present is nothing, but the echoes of my journey reverberate in the stillness of the night.

How I used to see this city was different; the towering skyscrapers and shimmering lights seemed like a fortress of opportunity. If I look back in time, I was confident about myself, but I never pictured myself as moving from the kitchen of a restaurant to the polished corridor of a corporate empire.

But was that all easy?

• • • • • • •

My first job was more like the first taste of survival; nonetheless, it was about 'survival of the fittest.' I often hear the clatter of dishes, the grill sizzle, and fellow colleagues' laughter echoing in my ears. Honestly, I like it. In fact, I love how I am still connected with my past, and it is a bit surprising that my memories are fresh, and I feel like I am in that moment. I was a waiter, a sweeper, a server—I was a multi-tasker. I was called for work, and I had to obey the manager. I never said no—because I knew that I would have to balance to survive in this city. Navigating through the chaos of the restaurant and the aroma of freshly cooked meals, I learned the value of hard work and resilience. But I never complained. In the initial days, I used to find it difficult, but then I used to enjoy the chaos. I learned it the hard way, but here is a piece of advice.

"Enjoy your work; if you don't enjoy working, you will never be able to get past your working hours."

Every other person was a philosopher, and I, being a young soul, used to take away something from everyone.

I remember it was peak winter season, and I was under the weather but had to work because, in winter, we used to get good tips because of the rush at the restaurant. I was balancing a tray of orders, and I heard someone say,

"In the chaos, find your way, and that's the key to the door of opportunities.

I turned around, but no one was there; it was just a regular scene of the restaurant. I don't know why, but the words became my mantra as I faced the challenges of serving demanding customers and balanced my way through getting a job that resonated with my qualifications.

• • • • • • •

If I come to think of it, the restaurant eventually became my training ground. It taught me the art of multitasking and also the importance of having a work—no matter how small. While working at the restaurant, I made my way toward learning ethics, dedication, and a sense of responsibility. Basically, in the kitchen, I learned the ingredients to succeed. Yes, if I think the job at the restaurant was not something big, it was a stepping stone in my journey. The struggle continued as I finally secured a job in the corporate world. It was a huge transition as if I had stepped into an entirely different world. The dimensions were different; the polished floors and the aesthetic office space carried a number of stories.

Acronyms, jargon, unwritten rules—it was not like I had a monumental job but an ordinary position in a grand scheme. But, I was immersed in the wisdom technicalities shared by colleagues during an important conversation. A plethora of learning, I was absorbing something new every minute.

I remember an incident clearly, and it was at that point that I made a decision to not give up at any point of time. I had a task to complete and immersed myself in a pile of files. And I heard, "Adaption is the key to survival; learn to follow the change, and you will find your way."

Somehow, the words became my light, wanting me to transform the ordinary into something extraordinary. The tasks on my desk were a routine, but everything changed its meaning, and the mantra of adaptation infused in each moment; it gave me a purpose. It was not about the nature of the job but it was about the evolution to climb the ladder.

• • • • • • •

As I prepared the reports, attended meetings, and carried the challenges of corporate life side by side, I learned every day. The mere ordinary tasks became opportunities for growth, and every day was a chance to refine my skills. In that flow of the office routine, I somehow managed to discover the key to success.

For me, "It is not about mastering the tasks you are assigned; it is about the ability to adapt and evolve from the ever-shifting currents."

And with that, my ordinary job turned into a process. I looked for the space for innovation and personal development. I made my ordinary designation extra-ordinary through the lens of adaptation and transformed my outlook of the daily grind. I made myself visible; I made sure that I was heard.

· · · · · · ·

As I look back, the mantra that I kept closed not only shaped my approach toward my work but also laid the foundation for my exploration of connectivity and technology. The ordinary became the training ground. I navigated my way through adaptation, resilience, and a mindset that would prove invaluable. The mindset took me to another arena, the ups and downs of connectivity into a brave new world.

The reflection to the past it always reminds me of a quote that resonates with my journey:

"In chaos, there is an opportunity."

• • • • • • •

Dear readers, every challenge has a potential turning point. But, during difficult times, we just want to get out of it, and we miss the areas of growth. The restaurant job and the corporate life became my array of experiences that also shaped my journey. From the clattering of the dishes to the hum of the lights, each phase had a role in shaping the person I am now. The struggles, the late-night works, working double; each contributed to resilience and growth.

Little did I know that these would become the foundation of exploration of connectivity and technology that awaited me. The lessons that I learned in the restaurant and the corporate corridors served as guiding principles.

• • • • • • •

For me, it was not about how big the job was; my first working experience in the corporate world was indeed a stepping stone, and soon it became the staircase to success. As a corporate beginner, the initial phase seemed daunting. Later on, all the acronyms and jargon made sense. The unwritten rules became pathways waiting to be accepted. Armed with the wisdom snatched from the polished corridors, and I was determined.

During the starting days, it was not like climbing the corporate ladder but felt like climbing a mountain. With each challenge, I embraced change and welcomed more challenges as opportunities for growth.

• • • • • • •

One day, it all changed; I was visible to people. It was one of the defining moments. I had been waiting for this opportunity all this time. I was entrusted with a project demanding my expertise and leadership skills. The assigned task was an opportunity to prove myself, and it ultimately became a strategy for success. As the project picked up speed, I found myself taking the lead. I navigated through dynamic challenges with my team and marked a successful ending.

That's how I got the space, with time promotions following each one, marking a new height in my climb.

I used to call it a "corporate summit."

All those acronyms, jargons, and unwritten rules now seemed like familiar companions.

The ability to lead, innovate, and adapt became my signature. Success was not about reaching at the top, but it was about learning through the journey. The change shaped me into a leader. The ordinary became extraordinary as I stood tall at the corporate summit.

As time went by, and my path in this renewed world developed, I became trapped within its complicated system of interconnectedness. Technology advancements changed the physical state of life and created a complicated mesh that interconnected every aspect of our lives. I was enveloped in one seamless array of connectivity from when I woke up to when my eyes closed.

• • • • • • •

In this brave new world of connectivity, a wealth of benefits emerged. Instant communication with anyone, anywhere, became a priceless asset. The digital space opened up networking opportunities, collaborating, and sharing knowledge on an unprecedented scale. Connectivity, professional and personal, around the world and to get a technical moment's notice on any subject under the sun.

The workplace changed radically. Remote collaboration tools allowed teams to operate effectively even without the restrictions of being in close physical proximity. I remembered how hard it was in the early days to send out job applications and go through interviews. Now, the digital world provided a wealth of opportunities where skills and requirements met in an electronic dance between employers and job seekers.

But as the connectivity web grew bigger, so did its shadows. Information overload became a constant headache. The more I became connected, the harder it was for me to distinguish between what mattered and what didn't.

• • • • • • •

Constant connectivity masked social isolation. While being immersed in a digital sea of faces and voices, the authentic bond between people seemed to fade away. Face-to-face conversations lost its uniqueness and magic, giving way to the efficiency of digital communications. But, the very notion of this interconnected world was paradoxical to me as I questioned whether relationships formed over screens were authentic.

In this journey up and down with connectivity, I dealt with the duality technology brought into my life. It opened doors to opportunities and made a level of convenience possible, which was unimaginable in the past on one hand. Conversely, it threw the shadow of information overload and a feeling that he was disconnected from reality.

So, as I was scrutinizing this dichotomy, it started to dawn on me that the essence of harmony lies in finding a middle ground. The web of connectivity was intricate and multi-faceted navigation that required mindfulness. On one hand, the benefits were apparent, but it was inevitable to avoid falling into pits.

I will get deeper into this intricately connected reality and look at how it affects our mental health relationships and what is being human in an era where technology takes precedence. The journey through the highs and lows of connectivity was just starting, fortitude and personal evolution in an environment built around its own pulse.

• • • • • • •

Chapter 3

Echoes of Simplicity: Nostalgia in Hometown Harmony

Dear readers,

I have struggled a lot in my life, and honestly, nothing comes easily. You have to pay a price at some point. But when there are struggles, you get to experience the essence of life.

Now, let me take you back to the town—I call home.

An ordinary town with an unknowing pure spirit, not divided by digitalization. A town which is far away from the trends of technology. As I write about my hometown, I can feel the warmth of the community that is cherished by simplicity and connection. The pace of life in my town is not dictated by the ticking of digital clocks but rather by the rhythm of shared moments and communal experiences.

The coffee shop—it is more like a gathering place for the people of the town. Literally a hub of conversation. People from all walks of life, sitting and sipping on their coffees, engaged in focused discussions. The absence of smartphones away from digital distractions fostered an environment which gave birth to genuine connections.

· · · · · · ·

I belonged to the school of the town; it lacked the latest technological gadgets, but it resonated with the passionate teachers and students. We did not have a smartboard, just a blackboard; for us, it was the ultimate source of knowledge. We learners collaborated in person, shared ideas, and supported academic dreams without the need for online platforms.

The job opportunities were not announced via the digital board, the jobs were discovered through networking and the community. Personal recommendations were given based on a shared understanding of one's skills and character. The economy of the town flourished by trust and personal connections.

The town was simply undivided, and the social participation was not done on social media platforms. Events were not created on social media but broadcasted via word of mouth. Festivals, celebrations, gatherings—a time for the entire town to come together.

• • • • • • •

As I transitioned from this haven to the glitzy city, I carried with me the lessons of my hometown. I had values of my community, the human connection, and the shared experiences.

Now that I look back—now that I am also surrounded by digitalization; I realize the damage done by digitalization. My transition was not smooth, but I had a command over the values, and I appreciated the human connections. The contrasts between my hometown's simplicity and the city's digital dazzle unfolded in many areas.

Everywhere I turned, heads were down, fingers tapping on screens, and conversations drowned in the pings of notifications. Honestly, I am done with this 'PING.' I missed the face-to-face dialogues and tried hard to fit in for the online validation.

∙ ∙ ∙ ∙ ∙ ∙ ∙

Soon, I became used to the 'Pings' because I became one of them. The ease of connection came at a cost; I lost life through the lens of a smartphone to the lens of personal observation.

In my wandering through the bright city streets, I missed the simplicity of common assemblies where individuals were truly present and absorbed in a world without machines. The bustle of the city seemed to leave no room for the relaxed conversations and joint fun that was typical of my hometown.

With the awareness of this digital influence in my life, nostalgia for true interaction seemed to dissolve within the maelstrom of modern technology. The values ingrained in my community became an anchor, an epitome of what truly mattered amidst the bright lights and pleasure provided by the city.

• • • • • • •

Influence vs Illusion

In this book, I will be honest with all my readers, as I truly want you to relate to my journey.

The realization that there is a digital divide, due to which there is a business, does not come to me easily.

The day I returned to the town that I once called home after being consumed by the city's shimmering. I stepped on the streets and felt comfort infused with the memories of the past. I was eager and anxious to reconnect with the community that made me who I am.

But reality hit me hard, which redefined my perspective on the digital landscape.

The day I returned to my hometown after being engulfed by the glitz and glam of the city was a revelation. As I stepped onto the familiar streets, the air infused with memories, I was eager to reconnect with the community that had shaped my values. Little did I know that reality would hit me with a force that would redefine my perspective on the digital landscape.

• • • • • • •

Walking through the town, I felt an unknown wind hitting; the town has subtle changes. The coffee shop—I was crazy even to think that it would be the same. To my horror, it had few young people engrossed in their smartphones, not having a real-time conversation. The shared discussions have taken a back seat to the allure of digital distractions.

It was curiosity that directed me to the town library—the place where I spent most of my time. The old computers I had logged into previously several years ago were there, their antique monitors apparently resistant to the velocity of technological development.

∙ ∙ ∙ ∙ ∙ ∙ ∙

They seemed like they had an agreement with time, not moving. When I saw the librarian, a familiar figure from the past, she looked at me in a way that she remembered me. Keeping the condition of the library in my mind, an old joke came out of me. "So, if I may say so, it appears that the computers have perfected temporal travel; they've been here since my dinosaur days!" I laughed sarcastically as a hint of laughter invaded my senses surrounding me when, indeed, nothing had changed.

The librarian even played along, her eyes twinkling. And these antiques? They get the job done or at least try. We could not but smile because we shared memories, and familiarity brought us together.

'Nothing has changed except this,' she said, referring to a faded chair in the corner with her smile. This chair has become its own character; more suspense and drama have unfolded in this setting than in your average Blockbuster movie. If only it could speak, it'd be the talk on every literary show by now!

The chair, now kept in the corner, was actually the chair of the librarian, which thankfully changed to a good foam-padded surfaced chair.

We laughed at the idea of the chair in the library telling its stories and making it silent witness to all these unfolding narratives. The conversation provided a welcome pause in the revelation of an unchanged library, which served as a reminder that even within stagnant technology, there was still humanity and laughter.

I conversed with old friends and new acquaintances, the stories unfolding as they did, however, despite sharing computers at the library, patiently waiting for their turn to get online resources. Job hunting and education opportunities remained full of hurdles that were brought about by limitations in internet access.

∙∙∙∙∙∙∙

As I engaged with the community, I heard stories of missed job opportunities and unrealized potential. Talented artists struggled to showcase their work beyond local exhibitions, and budding programmers faced obstacles in honing their skills without reliable internet access. The digital divide was not just a concept but a tangible force shaping the opportunities available to individuals in my hometown.

In one moment, a student shared their dreams of pursuing higher education but lacked online resources to prepare for entrance exams. The words lingered in the air, echoing the frustration of countless others who faced barriers to educational advancement due to the uneven distribution of technology.

As I left the library that day, the image of those eager students waiting for their turn at the outdated computers stayed with me. The story of my hometown became a personal lens through which I saw the profound impact of unequal access to technology on education, job opportunities, and social participation.

My hometown where over time, I could hear laughter on library floors cracking beneath shared jokes and stories that would never die out that is when change started coming. The library's ancient computers acted as mute spectators to the elapsing of time, but it wasn't just the machines that were trapped in history; access to the digital universe was provided from years ago.

• • • • • • •

As I traveled through acquainted streets, something within me started perceiving indicators of the digital divide that had silently slipped into my community. Recreation for the job market, once extensive, is now limited by dint of digital restriction. With no continuous connectivity, the light of education became darkened. Face-to-face interactions had allowed the communal spirit to flourish until it confronted these shadows of a divide that further ruined social involvement.

My birthplace was not the only one in this story. Accounts from nearby municipalities depicted a similar portrait. In these neighborhoods, the absence of technology had become an invisible barrier, slowing down their travel to progress and development. The sound of job applications resounded in old ways, and the footsteps of learning bumped against obstacles without the measuring stick provided by technology.

In one town, the vibrant hustle and bustle of its local market was dampened by businesses desperately fighting for survival against the silence of e-commerce. In another, splashes of color from community events were dulled by the lack of digital media to extend their impact. The differences were not only in the infrastructure but on how opportunities flourished from being connected digitally.

To look back on the changes that my hometown and neighboring areas went through in recent years, I could see how this digital divide cast its shadows; it unveiled very subtle yet far-reaching damage to the place. The glue that was once the essence of these towns' undivided spirit wore invisible wounds inflicted by limited digital access.

• • • • • • •

The harm was consequently not visible in the form of a collapsing structure or a deteriorated road, but rather through what had been lost: missed opportunities and dreams that were never realized whispered from testimonies. The flourishing job scene had been damaged, and the absence of digital platforms reduced access to jobs.

The effects of the damage on education were obvious, reflecting on those students struggling to learn outside classrooms. However, the lack of a strong digital presence meant that resources for education were limited, and creativity was hampered by this limitation. The opportunities for growth.

The web of social platforms, entwined on communal meetings and shared experiences, now sagged in a parting that caused impotent relationships. These traces of the past were seen in dipping reverberation into squares and subdued excitement about events that did not extend beyond the boundaries.

As I interacted with people from these small towns, their stories created a collective story of the devastation that wreaked. Many gifted people, filled with possibilities, became constrained by the borders of digital space. Small business owners were hindered from growing their businesses beyond local borders, and the young desired want even when opportunities appeared unreachable without enough Internet sources.

Influence vs Illusion

• • • • • • •

Walking through the streets that once shared human connections, I could feel the digital divide in physical space. While my hometown has not lost its cohesiveness, the shortage of digital sources has become an obstacle to progress for many. The freedoms I had assumed in the city were few and far between here, and the scars of the digital divide were etched on their attempt to level the playing field.

It provoked a wave of reflections between the current situation and what I saw in my hometown. I realized that the united soul of this community was strong, but a deficiency in digital assets created an issue that needed to be addressed.

The realization hit me: while I was navigating the corporate world with the mantra of adaptation, a significant portion of my hometown was grappling with the challenges of access. The digital divide was not just a statistic; it was a lived experience for many.

• • • • • • •

Chapter 4

Echoes of Progress: The Dance of Tradition and Innovation

As I lay down in the comforting arena of my home, the familiar surroundings seemed to be introspective. The ambient lights painted a tranquil scene, and the gentle warmth on the walls witnessed the intensity of my life. In that quiet moment, I reclined and let my thoughts wander. The hum of the outside world began to fade. The muted sounds of the night created a contemplation.

The quietness was taking over me, with every breath, I found myself drawn into the sanctuary of my reflections. As I gazed at the ceiling, a pyramid of thoughts took residence. A stepping stone into the stairs of memories and musings. It was in this cocoon of solitude that I began to unravel my experiences. A journey of mind sparked by the simple act of reclining and letting the stories unfold.

Struggling was fate for all of us——I had a hard time achieving what I have now, but if I look back in the past, I can relate to the past, present, and future too.

A small industrial town between the hills, the rhythmic machinery marked the dawn of a new era. The promise of progress echoed through the air as the first automated loom was introduced to the local textile factory.

Among the workers was my grandfather, a proficient weaver who had spent decades perfecting this craft through his nimble hands and keen eyes. When the automated loom was presented, people reacted with a combination of wonder and intrigue. The town hummed with talk of efficiency and heightened production, every twist of the cog in the automated loom representing a step toward progress.

However, for my grandfather, the first days were a ballet of tradition and innovation. The constant drone of the machine became a kindred spirit to his trade, and now conjoined with them were shuttles and looms merging into an ordered symphony that was automation. The productivity gains and simplified operations were tangible, shining a bright light on the factory's future as well as that of its town.

As the mechanical loom smoothly produced elaborate designs, my grandfather was swept away in a tornado of transformation. Whereas the factory once relied on craftsmen's skilled hands, it now embraced mechanical efficiency. But the shadows of automation were hidden under a glare of progress. The town rejoiced in the higher production, and optimism regarding a brighter future ruled all talks.

But, as time went by, the shadows grew longer. In the workforce, shifts came to be apparent also in the once-flourishing community of craftsmen. The young generation that was so excited to learn the fine art of weaving now finds itself attracted by the lure of working in industrial mechanized looms. The soothing noise of progress now carried hints of doubt.

· · · · · · ·

My grandfather's personal aspects evolved gradually. The traditional loom, which he had mastered so well, became a thing of the past by being overshadowed by automation's efficiency. The fine touches, the delicate nuances that only a master's hands could instill, began to wither before advancement. The shadows that were previously hidden are now seen, tempering the light of human workers.

This personal story represents the larger narrative in early automation days, where there were promises of progress with complex realities associated with transition of workforce. Behind every cog of the wheel, there is always a unique story engraved with intricate details of evolution and transformation.

The backstory basically extends and reminds me of the early days of automation. The efficiency was championed as the herald of progress. The era resonated with the hum of the machines in the majority of the factories. In those days, everything felt like magic; a promise of enhanced productivity and streamlined operation took over the shadows that automation would cast on the human force.

∙ ∙ ∙ ∙ ∙ ∙ ∙

Influence vs Illusion

Imagine an industrialized landscape dotted with gigantic factories in which workers labored hand-in-hand alongside new machines. It emerged from a time of the relentless drive toward efficiency and consequently led to automation in all parts. The appeal of higher productivity and lower costs inspired a mania that swept over factories like an inspirational breath of air.

Seismic changes swept through the human workforce, leaving in its wake a wave of change that altered communities and lifestyles. With skilled craftsmen and laborers, once the beating heart of production, now have their space on the floor with machines that could work tirelessly without ever making a mistake. This flipside was revealed when workers saw the inevitable displacement of their jobs.

The back story gives the feelings of this industrial revolution that took to hearts who were there. Workers also tried to combine pride in technologies with uncertainty about their roles, which were fluctuating as a result of technological progress. The dance between humans and machines began to turn these factories, places once full of dynamic human energy, into stages.

But the siren call of progress was irresistible. The story winds its way through the automation's pioneers, people who created an image of a future where efficiency would liberate mankind from work bonds. The technology of development buzzed with hope, and it became a prelude to change that would reverberate through the halls of history.

· · · · · · ·

The vibrant cityscape with pulsating innovation, I think about the ethics of innovation. In the wake of technological progress, caution and reflection urge us to navigate the crossroads with an understanding of the consequences that innovation can bring.

The digital age, where promises of convenience with the tendrils of ethical ambiguity. The individuals enthusiastically embraced the digital realm. Standing at the crossroads of progress and morality, where the dazzling possibilities of technology also illuminate the shadows of ethical dilemmas.

With the emergence of digital age, data became currency with which innovation engines were driven. But this digital treasure trove created moral dilemmas as the distinction between usefulness and invasion became more obscured. Turning our attention to the intricacies of data privacy, we unravel how innovation appears at times, stepping on these individual tendrils. I think about the cases of people in this crossfire where convenience meets at an odd angle with personal information.

As wondrous as Artificial Intelligence is and could be in redefining the limits of humankind, it also comes with its fair share of ethical dilemmas. The story takes place in the areas of machine learning, algorithms, and the enormous power that AI gives to decision-making processes. The process of moving through realistic situations allows us to navigate the maze of ethical considerations and wonder about what we should be accountable for as intelligent systems developers. The chapter struggles over the changing understanding of AI ethics and enforcing a moral compass to guide artificial intelligence.

∙ ∙ ∙ ∙ ∙ ∙ ∙

Influence vs Illusion

The machines of automation grind on with an unflinching ferocity, and the human workforce walks towards being renewed. It turns the spotlight on ethical issues of automation rising when efficiency meets with joblessness. We follow the stories of individuals whose livelihoods will be sacrificed as we delve into this highly complex dance between progress and responsibility, uncovering issues of morality from a workforce transformed by automation.

· · · · · · ·

The conflict between progress and liability captures the limelight in the relentless mechanization. The story progresses, revealing the nuances of ethical concerns that arise from the collision of machine efficiency with the possibility of human joblessness.

As the machines mercilessly rake on, the human workforce is faced with a moment of rebirth—a metamorphosis that is not free of ethical conundrums. The story goes deeper into the lives of those who put their livelihoods at stake despite knowing that it would lead to a vicious cycle between development and responsibility.

Behind the scenes of efficiency gains, a harsh truth is revealed. Job displacement transcends a mere hypothetical question; it becomes a reality threatening the livelihood of skilled craftsmen and laborers. The human cost of automation is exposed as communities have to deal with the aftermath of progress.

∙ ∙ ∙ ∙ ∙ ∙ ∙

The story of these people whose abilities once allowed the production to stand unshaken is being told in the narrative. With the increasing use of machines, the ethical considerations of such a change start to show. The existential questions of accountability, societal effects, and the moral obligation to deliver on the consequences of automation rest heavily on the minds of those steering the direction of progress.

The ethical scenery also covers the broader consequences on humans. It goes into the wider societal issues, discussing how the gains from automation can be shared. With the advent of the new workforce— of machines, issues of social justice and ethical responsibility are now in the spotlight.

As a human experience, dilemmas, and the changing landscape of the robotic world. It makes one contemplate the duties arriving alongside technological progress and the importance of managing development working with a solid consciousness of its moral parts.

Chapter 5

Navigating the Digital Divide: Evolution of Talent Acquisition

I vividly remember the early days of my career, and when I reflect on the corporate journey navigating the ebbs and flows of success, the job market has undergone a major metamorphosis. Yes, I struggled a lot to achieve the levels on which I am today. But, the corridors of power and decision-making, where I now stand, bear witness to the transformative impact of technology and how employees are not recruited.

The interview, selection, and recruitment process back in my days was a traditional setting. Face-to-face interaction, and not just the qualifications on a resume, was the essence of a candidate. But, with the rise of technology, the professional setting, the competition, everything made a shift. Video interviews, artificial intelligence, resume screenings, and virtual assessment tools ushered a new era of talent acquisition.

· · · · · · ·

The algorithms are the new kings; there are new identifying patterns and skills that have eluded the human eye. Video interviews have become commonplace and transcend geographical barriers, allowing employers to evaluate candidates around the globe. The charm of the interview room, unfolding a number of candidates in a confused state and nervous energy, has expanded into a digital space. The virtual meetings and assessments shape the first impressions of the potential hires.

But where is the human touch?

I remember being interviewed by three different people and then a panel interview in which there were around six people. But now, the human touch is nowhere to be found.

The algorithms, the artificial intelligence—are sorting out the resume, defining the candidate, and lastly, being selected by AI.

Artificial intelligence has become the gatekeeper of talent.

· · · · · · ·

In the times of modern recruitment, when algorithms and artificial intelligence are controlling talent, a journey before conventional resume takes on is a digitized odyssey. The formerly static sheet of paper undergoes a metamorphosis as it turns into a dynamic entity venturing through the virtual universe where lines of code dissection qualifications, skills, and experiences with algorithmic accuracy.

When a resume moves toward digital, it faces its first checkpoint—automated resume screening. Biased-free and with everlasting objectivity, algorithms rave through the document, unraveling keywords, qualifications, and professional accomplishments. This first meeting with artificial intelligence is a critical point at which the digital gatekeepers decide whether to move a resume to another stage or into the deepness of digital obscurity.

Luck only comes for the few who evade this algorithmic scrutiny, and their odyssey is enhanced. The virtual interviews based on artificial intelligence, hence proving to be the platform where the essence of a candidate is not only heard but also evaluated. Algorithms analyze facial expressions, vocal tone, and even the nuances of language with a view to predicting cultural fit and communication skills. It is the time when the digital world peels the layers off of a candidate's personality and hands a synthesized version to employers.

Influence vs Illusion

· · · · · · ·

Influence vs Illusion

The selection stage is the ultimate of this digital audition. In this case, the algorithms go through all data points and produce a shortlist of candidates that best fit the position. The ultimate decision that used to be based only on human intuition is now also impacted by the computations and predictions made by artificial intelligence. Lines of code balance qualifications, soft skills, and cultural fit determine the path a candidate's career will take forward.

History, however, does not stay frozen in time anymore, and now, instead of the story of a resume, it is spoken by programs. It sets off on a digital odyssey dependent on the cold calculations executed by artificial intelligence. While dealing with this terrain in my corporate position, the synergy between human instinct and digital efficacy becomes a linchpin of redefining employment market lands. Between algorithms and human decision makers is a story that will unravel, where we see complex relationships connect to develop talent acquisition in an era of artificial intelligence.

• • • • • • •

Influence vs Illusion

In the dim corners of the contemporary employment map an unprecedented act is taking place which will define the future of work for years to come. It is an account rooted in the subtleties that permeate technological influence and attempts to untangle the complex weave of change as it relates to modern employment.

∙ ∙ ∙ ∙ ∙ ∙ ∙

Influence vs Illusion

Sitting at the intersection of traditional office settings and virtual worlds, remote work arises as a dominating topic. The office is no longer defined by the boundaries of a building but rather extends into virtual environments and embraces working remotely. The story discusses the role of technology in breaking down geographic barriers and how it enables people to contribute towards a global effort without entering an office building. This chapter goes through difficulties and benefits embedded into remote work, from virtual boardrooms to home offices.

A choir of flexibility and freedom emerges in the changing scene of work. By using real-life stories and examples, we explore a world of gig workers where digital platforms bring together freelancers who perform anything from the ordinary to the remarkable. The story cuts through the effect of the gig economy in disrupting traditional employment models by illustrating that today's work interactions are increasingly dictated on short-term engagements and project collaborations.

Technology, as a disruptive force in today's world of jobs, modifies the significance and nature of roles. My surroundings reveal stories about industries reconfigured by automation, artificial intelligence, and innovative technologies. The stories take us through manufacturing floors and corporate boardrooms, showing how the inexorable force of progress informs job opportunities, leaving some roles irrelevant whereas creating unimagined.

∙ ∙ ∙ ∙ ∙ ∙ ∙

It is rather an encounter that one person has had as a manifestation of how technology has disrupted the role of employment. Also, I remember a crucial turning point when my team went through the transition, incorporating automation and AI to optimize processes. The story of this change was about the implementation of the most advanced technologies and the human tales embroidered into the cloth of this digital transformation.

As the algorithms and automation became the focus, the apprehension from the workforce was quite visible. The threat of getting replaced and the undercurrents of uncertainties continued to hover in the air. This was also the time that I saw the resiliency and adaptability of my peers.

• • • • • • •

In the middle of the chaotic changes, a fellow, Sarah, personified innovation. Automation automated the mundane responsibilities, thereby turning her role into a metamorphosis. At first, she met hesitation, yet Sarah took the chance to reskill/upskill and adapt her work to the tasks that required human labor that is, creativity, critical thinking, and strategic decision-making.

Sarah's case became a miniature example of the larger story unraveling in industries worldwide. Certain parts of the job were automated; this did not render the job obsolete but rather reshaped the roles of the job. It became clear that, no matter how much technology can do repetitive work with accuracy, irreplaceable human qualities such as intuition, empathy, and creativity have found new ways to thrive.

•••••••

This personal account brought out how technology and human ingenuity are symbiotic. The threat of job disappearance became the platform for development and maturation. It was a reminder that, no matter how much technology disrupted the status quo, the human factor was irreplaceable.

From the sidelines of employment as a whole, the case of people such as Sarah signified a paradigm shift – from stories of jobs lost to stories of roles redefined. Human capabilities fused with technological advancements became a formidable phenomenon, establishing a story where learning and adaptability were the answers to surviving in the digital age.

∙ ∙ ∙ ∙ ∙ ∙ ∙

Influence vs Illusion

The idea that the future of work is not a foregone path that can be designed by technology alone comes back to me as I progress in this group of stories and experiences. It is a partnership dance between the digital and the human, where every step we take is governed by our decisions and the strength we show.

• • • • • • •

Influence vs Illusion

In the forthcoming chapters, I expect to look into more stories of adaptation, innovation, and the delicate ballet between man and machine in the dynamic world of work. Together, let us keep peeling away the layers of this fascinating story where the interplay between man and machine reshapes work boundaries and renders it professional.

• • • • • • •

Chapter 6

Virtual Realities: The Allure and Peril of Digital Escapism

Virtual reality, escapism, addiction—what are these?

A powerful force?

It is An inviting power that allows individuals to step beyond the boundaries of reality and immerse themselves in the alternate world.

Virtual reality, online communities, and explore the allure of escapism and potential shadows of addiction that hide within the digital landscape.

When I was struggling with the corporate ladder, artificial intelligence, and trying to make a space in this high-artificial world, I used to think;

"In the virtual world, I can be anyone, do anything. It's a break from the constraints of my everyday life."

As I strap on the virtual reality headset, the tangible world ultimately dissolves. It gives away the alternate reality where the possibilities are limitless.

I will be honest here; the exploration of virtual reality became a journey of human desire to escape from the complexities and challenges of real life.

The stories of individuals who find solace, adventure, and temporary comfort within the digital embrace of virtual reality.

In the mesmerizing landscapes of virtual reality, there lies a danger of addiction. And I have been a victim of this addition.

"It started as a way to unwind, to relax. But as soon as I found myself preferring the virtual over the real, it became an addiction I couldn't break."

Not just me, I have heard dozens of stories from different individuals who find themselves grappled by the web of digital escape.

Not just this, I have experienced dialogues with psychologists, experts, and also those who have experienced the shadows of addiction first-hand to shed light on the fine line between healthy escapism and perilous descent into the clutches of digital dependency.

• • • • • • •

My journey has not only limited to personal reflections, but it goes beyond. I've had dialogues with psychologists, field experts, and individuals who have battled addiction in real life. These dialogues have been enlightening excursions that point at the thin line separating healthy escapism from dangerous digital addiction.

Via these interactions, I have gained an understanding of the psychological mechanisms at work when it comes to our relationship with technology. The line between the states of responsible engagement in the digital realm for the purpose of relaxation and the risks of falling into an addictive state of mind has become more visible. Rather than the quantity of time spent on social media, it's all about engagement quality and its impact on psychological health.

I am now more conscious and aware of how my digital habits could have led to these inevitable encounters in my past life as well. They point to the demand for open dialogue about the dangers and development of approaches to create a balanced environment. Adding the voices of those who have dealt with addiction as real people and not mere statistics has brought a noted human element to the conversation, making it more of a collaborative initiative than a sole effort to discover the complex digital landscape.

Influence vs Illusion

In truth, these discussions have also come to be part of my continuing process, offering me wisdom that is more than what my personal reflections can provide. They are part of a larger storyline geared towards unraveling our relationship with technology, consequently creating a more informed and deliberate tech placement.

• • • • • • •

In the virtual world, individuals often try to discover a refuge from the stressors and challenges of their everyday lives. The heartfelt dialogues and personal narrative as we try to reveal the stories of positive escapism. The individuals see virtual reality and online communities as therapeutic spaces.

I would share my own experience:

"In this digital world, I found a place where my creativity could soar and where I could heal from the scars of reality."

Within the shadows of negative consequences loom, and in the pursuit of escape, they find themselves engraved in the web of addiction and detachment from reality.

• • • • • • •

I remember having a conversation with a psychologist who experienced the darker side of escapism. The insight of the conversation was something like:

"It started as a break, a way to unwind. As I spent more time in the virtual world, I began to lose touch with the actual life, the real life. Yes, it is a thin line, and I crossed it without even realizing it."

Is there a thin line?

Yes, there is a thin line that separates the positive escapism from the darkest part. For a better understanding, I have had dialogues with mental health professionals and individuals who have successfully balanced the virtual realities with the demands of real life.

And honestly, without the help of mental health professionals, I would have never gained the wisdom. This is something that I learned from the entire narrative.

• • • • • • •

"The key is to balance; escapism can be a tool for relaxation, but it is also essential to remain grounded in the real world; it is about finding the right harmony between the digital and actual life.

In the ongoing exploration of virtual reality, escapism, and the shadows of addiction. Let's get into some personal details. I would love to shed light on the phenomena of escaping the complexities of real life and the subsequent pitfalls of digital dependency.

As the virtual reality headset is strapped on, I somehow dive deeper into the limitless possibilities of the alternate reality, acknowledging the initial that promises a break from the constraints of everyday life. A journey that began as a means to unwind and relax but gradually transformed into an addiction that proved challenging to break.

· · · · · · ·

I am plunging deeper into the endless possibilities of an alternative reality, the initial attraction promising an escape from the realities of day-to-day life. The initial purpose of this trip was to destress, but fortunately or unfortunately, that is not what holds true today.

Consequently, the immersive character of the virtual world first offered respite—a place away from real-life problems where I could retreat and hence discover even what I had never dared to conceive. Nevertheless, the limits between fun and habit dissolved as the digital worlds turned out to be more and more enthralling, vexing me deeper into their embrace.

The hunt for rest became a constant desire for virtual departure, paving the way for an attempt to free myself from the claws of this internet dependency. What was first meant as a breath of fresh air from reality now proved a formidable constraint, as the virtual world seemed to get an increasing grip on users.

When facing the digital web, I realize the need for consciousness and a constructive attempt to broach a new relationship between me and technology. The road that started as the call for freedom now forces me to

Influence vs Illusion

be thoughtful, urging me to revise the borderlines between the virtual and the real and restore equilibrium between escapism and mindfulness.

· · · · · · ·

I have shared personal experiences and echoed the sentiments of countless individuals who found themselves entangled in the web of digital escape. Through dialogues with psychologists, experts, and those who have first-hand experience with the shadows of addiction, the narrative seeks to illuminate the fine line between healthy escapism and the perilous descent into digital dependency.

In exploring virtual worlds, individuals often seek refuge from the stressors and challenges of their everyday lives.

The shadows of negative consequences loom as the pursuit of escape sometimes leads to addiction and detachment from reality. The narrative navigates through these complexities, highlighting the dual nature of escapism and the delicate balance required to avoid its darker manifestations.

∙∙∙∙∙∙∙

Chapter 7

Pixels and Paradoxes: Navigating the Social Media Landscape

As we dive deeper into the digital landscape, the virtual and the tangible converge in rays of pixels and emotions, and we confront the paradox of social media.

A connection that coexists with isolation, self-expression intertwines with self-doubt, and a digital paradise that shows the shadows of the realities of mental well-being.

Social Media Paradox?

"It is a virtual funhouse; sometimes you are laughing, sometimes you are lost, and every now and then, you wonder if the mirror is playing a prank on your selfie."

Yes, social media has an intriguing effect. It's somewhat like a paradox effect. The illusion of acceptance and validation detrimentally affects one's self-esteem in reality.

I would explain it: portraying what we want people to see and expecting 'likes' in return seems to promise rewarding feelings of accomplishment and connectivity.

Social media is a confusing state of mind, where friendships flourish, and the success of stories abound. But as we peer behind the pixels, the paradoxical nature of this digital world, I believe that I have gotten insights into the construction of digital facades.

• • • • • • •

Social media is a new reality; relationships unfold while a triumphant narrative overflows on a screen where pixels meet the perfect picture. Nevertheless, looking beyond the digital chaos, the meta-paradoxical nature of this process can be observed. Through this journey, I've learned about the fine-grained structure of virtual elements. Nevertheless, what is portrayed on social media platforms is the stories handpicked, and the characters scratched that conceal the complexities and efforts that hide beneath. It's a world where you show you're successful and celebrate institutions. The authenticity of the portrayal, however, can be very illusive. Whilst searching for likes and shares the genuine meaning behind the perfected pictures can get lost.

The working of social media left me wondering what the real essence of these digital links is. Are they raw depictions of lives experienced or pristine fragments purposefully chosen for public view?

Contemplating flourishing friendships and storylines engineered for the sake of success makes us look into the reasons that help us craft our internet profiles.

This investigation has paved the way for a far more discriminating way in which I do my own practices within the digital sphere. It is a recollection that despite plenty of common stories, there is a necessity for being actual, true, and sincere connection. The insights into building digital facades are a call to look at this sphere with a critical mindset, search for the underlying significance, and acknowledge the rough and unedited traits of real-life interactions.

∙∙∙∙∙∙∙

Social media is full of success stories, connections, and narratives, but an extremely detailed and complex exploration reveals how the digital façade is woven. Pixels and profiles, at times, reflect this dualistic nature that speaks volumes about the making and unmaking of these self-composed online characters.

Social media has become a platform where people exhibit perfectionism in everything they do. Then comes another story that unfolds silently through the choice of filters and angles for perfect lives and outstanding accomplishments. Nonetheless, the more I explored this virtual world, I discovered its own contradictions lying beneath its surface.

Every glamorous post or polished image carries with it a subtext of vulnerability. Those platforms set up to display triumphs are thus turned into spaces where individuals can come to terms with dicey situations they face in their lives. Such talks surrounding mental health, personal battles, and authenticity quests interrupt the glossy exterior, exposing real-life human experiences stripped down to their simplest forms.

Influence vs Illusion

While friendships grow and achievements seem endless on social media, it paradoxically metamorphoses itself into a trap for comparing oneself with others.

∙ ∙ ∙ ∙ ∙ ∙ ∙

In the ever-stretching social media era where friendships dawn and successes multiply, a contradiction arises — the platform subtlety transitions into a never-ending loop of self-comparison. Within the jubilee of networking and achievements, the core of social media goes beyond people's self to instill heavy comparisons of oneself to others.

Curated online narratives and video highlight reels that feature on these digital spaces often become the measuring sticks of personal success and happiness. You can easily fall into the habit of comparing your life with what seems to be the perfect images and stories others have to offer. The continuous encounter with the accomplishments of others and their seemingly flawless lives makes one feel unsatisfactory because he [or she] cannot keep up with the impossibly high standards of success.

The ambiguous nature of social media, however, warrants some deep thinking about the emotional destruction that comparison can bring about. It touches the very core of the platform, asking whether it is really creating true connection or is even unintentionally breeding competition and self-doubt.

In traveling this digital terrain, I have learned the necessity of nurturing a positive mindset and of accepting my route as a personal one. Social media is a very powerful tool that brings people together for bonding and celebration but it also demands an effort to resist the attraction of comparison. It is a wake-up call that beneath the curated narratives hide the complexities of real lives, and complete satisfaction is achieved by following your path as opposed to measuring it against others' digital phase.

• • • • • • •

Influence vs Illusion

In the era of social media, the desire for validation of likes and comments greatly influences how people interact. As I delved into the intricacies of seeking approval in the world, I discovered a balance between genuine connections and the potential pitfalls of relying on external validation. It's fascinating to witness both the sense of empowerment and vulnerability that arise from measuring one's worth based on metrics.

Taking a look beyond the surface I came across stories that often go untold amidst the facade of social media. Behind those curated images lies a reality filled with moments and candid narratives that diverge from what is presented to our digital audience. This disconnect serves as a reminder of how perception in the realm can differ from actual reality.

· · · · · · ·

Social paradox, and almost every individual is bound by it.

"Every post is more like a stroke on a wall that conceals as much as it reveals."

I feel social media is both a stage and a mask, and its illusions can be complex.

For some, it serves as a lifeline, connecting individuals across distances and also fostering a sense of belonging. The paradox emerges as the juxtaposition of digital connection and also the undercurrents of isolation that can permeate these virtual spaces.

I won't be lying if I quote it like:

"I have friends all over the world, yet the more connected I am online, the more I feel a sense of isolation in my offline world. Yes, it is a peculiar paradox."

• • • • • •

The longing for authenticity amidst contrived content as the story continues to unfold. Dialogues with content creators and influencers highlight the delicate balance between crafting a digital persona and the pursuit of genuine self-expression:

"In a world where filters, hashtags, and trends are everywhere, the real test is living authentically as your unapologetic self. It's navigating imperfections in this digitalized environment effectively."

The expedition ends with the contemplation of how to preserve equilibrium in relation to social media. Dialogues with psychologists and digital well-being experts provide practical insights, offering a roadmap to navigate the paradox and foster a positive online experience:

Social media does not have to be abandoned; it has to embrace a mindful, intentional relationship. Setting boundaries, real-world connection development, and digital well-being must formulate three pillars of equilibrium between wireless life.

Let me peel off various layers of Social Media Paradox, understanding their paradigm between connection and isolation as well as self-expression and doubt. The unusual way in which It is organized and helps to replace the digital cover, making readers doubt and reflect on their relationship with social media.

· · · · · · ·

Chapter 8

Guardians of the Digital Realm: A Tale of Cybersecurity

Allow me to narrate a story that will explain how I feel about the digital destruction.

Once upon a time in the interconnected kingdom of Cyberspace, where the information flowed like a river. Personal information was protected as a treasure and a target for forces.

Matt lived in the cyber world, and in this landscape of the internet lived a digital evil named Malwarex. He used to constantly seek vulnerabilities to exploit. In the world of the internet, digital destruction cause leaving a trail of dangers.

One day, Matt was calmly roaming around in the forest of online transactions there, he met a wise sage named Encryptra. Adorned in a cloak of encryption, he warned Matt about the dangers and importance of safeguarding personal information. Matt wanted to fortify the defenses against Malwarex and its minions. He took all the right steps, and first, he created a shield of strong passwords, each guarding the gates of digital accounts. Little did Matt know, Malwarex was cunning; he tried to breach the fortress of information through the gates of social media, where personal stories and details were shared freely. The open profiles and opinions of the people of this cyber world gave leverage to Malwarex to breach the information.

Matt, guided by Encryptra's light, learned the art of social media awareness, adjusting privacy settings, and minimizing the vulnerability to prying eyes.

∙∙∙∙∙∙∙

In the river of online transactions, Matt encountered the power of two-factor authentication. It was indeed a wise step that provided an additional layer of protection. Together, they forged an unbreakable bond that kept Malwarex at bay.

Matt kept on fighting against the ill intentions of Malwarex and in the way, found the power of secure internet browsing. He navigated through the suspicious websites and utilized the magic of VPNs along with them.

You know about VPNs (Virtual Private Networks).

• • • • • • •

In the quest for digital safety, Matt made sure to leave no stone unturned. And while he was struggling to protect the cyber world, he met the software update oracle, and there it hit the spot and became a magical potion that strengthened the digital world.

The climax of this story unfolds as Matt faces the final countdown. Armed with the knowledge gained from Encryptra, the strength of strong passwords, the guardianship of two-factor authentication, and the wisdom of secure internet browsing, Matt won the battle. The kingdom of cyberspace celebrated as Matt became the king of digital literacy.

∙ ∙ ∙ ∙ ∙ ∙ ∙

This was in the wake of Matt's victory in Cyberspace, a wake effect of consciousness and strength, the digital world was awakened. His digital quest story became a beacon, inspiring others to ponder over the necessity of safeguarding their virtual empires.

The cyber world, similar to the interdependent world we live in, reflects the hurdles in reality. The story of Matt's journey is employed as a symbol of the importance of digital privacy for our lives. It highlights the need to be proactive in protecting personal information in a world where the distinction between the physical and the digital is becoming increasingly indistinct.

The implied message in this story is a warning—a warning to be vigilant, educated, and proactive in protecting our digital realms. It is not just a fairy tale but a manual for the real world, where privacy and protection acquire utmost importance. Matt's story serves as a spark that lights up people to find out the weak points of their digital fortresses, set up defenses, and try to see the digital world through the lens of privacy.

Going further into the developing digital age, privacy, security, and vulnerability are not fantasies but realities. The story moves into a guide, revealing the significance of digital literacy and the adoption of sufficient information protection measures. It becomes a guide to mitigating the damages that come with the unprecedented growth of technology in the digital age.

• • • • • • •

Starting from this background, the story smoothly flows into the world of actual cases of digital destruction. Through case studies, the book highlights real-life situations of cyber threats, data breaches, and criminal acts that were costly to governments and individuals. The stories act as warning tales, illustrating the essential necessity of safe solutions for privacy and the associated risks of our digitalized lives.

As we move forward, we will go on to undo the layers of digital privacy, getting into tools, techniques, and issues associated with consumer privacy and physical safety, thereby building a better, safer, more secure digital world. Let us walk this path together, dear readers, into the digital age, trying to find a balance between technology and the right to your privacy.

• • • • • • •

Basically, the book is meant to link the incomprehensible space of the net and the demand for control over data and privacy issues. It emphasizes how the digital era brings levels of convenience, connectivity and information that are unparalleled as well as the increased fear of data misuse.

The whole point of this narrative is- the world has become a cyberspace mirrors the challenges faced in the real world. The importance of digital privacy in our interconnected lives lies in this world.

The quest for privacy, protection, and resilience is not a fictional narrative but rather a call to action in this real-world landscape of the internet.

The story carries a message related to digital destruction. Be vigilant, be informed, and be proactive in defending your digital world. This story was not just a fantasy but a guide for a reality where privacy and protection were the priority.

∙ ∙ ∙ ∙ ∙ ∙ ∙

This story goes with the tale of digital danger. It functions as a prompt to keep up to guard mode, knowledgeable and aggressive in the defence of our digital space.

What we have is no fiction but a story that provides guidance for a world where security and protection take precedence.

In digital landscape where it can be both charming and dangerous, the fiction speaks of the need of awareness of the risks which hide behind the pixels. It promotes a proactive approach in keeping personal data secure and perceptively, traversing the complex online landscape.

∙ ∙ ∙ ∙ ∙ ∙ ∙

The narrative is not only a form of amusement but is also an imperative lesson aimed at the need to keep hold of the volatile equilibrium between entanglement and perseverance. It triggers reflection on our digital behavior and how we can defend ourselves against it. With the narrative ensuing, it is now a call to arms, designating a viewpoint that considers privacy crucial while holding accountability of being a knowledgeable digital subject.

• • • • • •

In essence, the story provides more than just an imaginative respite – it becomes a symbol, lighting the path through the challenges of the present-day digital realm, where awareness, vigilance, and a proactive stance become the steering wheel defying any attempt to see our digital spaces desecrated.

With the development of technology, information has become a currency, but control over data and privacy issues are more crucial than ever in the digital era. In case the internet is like an unfathomable space; we are continuously in danger of seeing our private information take part in a mechanism that involves its misuse and potential digital devastation. The main goal of this book is to discuss the importance of protecting one's digital privacy and putting into practice adequate data protection measures that would reduce risks, which are brought about by the rapid growth in technology.

• • • • • •

The evolution brought the digital age with it, and along with it came unprecedented levels of convenience, connectivity, and information. Nevertheless, the advancements that came from this progress are countered by increased fear of personal data misuse. All spheres of our lives, including online purchases and even services related to social media, can become targets for privacy violations. The digitization of most areas of everyday life is exceptionally easy today, particularly when it comes to medical records and smart home devices that represent means for personal data protection as well as tools for invading one's private sphere.

· · · · · · ·

For a better idea of the magnitude, the book guides its readers to actual scenarios of digital destruction that left people and organizations victims of cyber threats, data breaches, and criminals. These case studies show how critical the lack of reliable solutions to protect privacy brings about undesirable outcomes.

• • • • • • •

Chapter 9

Dancing with Doubt: Navigating the Affair with AI

My dearest readers,

Let me reveal a secret, my relationship with AI has left me confused. In this bustling city, where progress echoed in every stress, I was trapped by the integration of artificial intelligence into everyday life.

As I navigate through the digital landscape, the sweet affair between AI and myself unfolded.

As I go into future implications toward which smart technologies are heading towards the future, one of such futuristic implication would be that smart technologies are so much intelligent in the sense that they anticipated my preferences, and it was from the intelligence artificial assistants will schedule to make working easier for me, while city infrastructure is optimizing my daily commute. These conveniences were the threads that effortlessly interwoven into my solemn, repetitious existence, lending to life a certain efficiency and seamlessness.

However, despite this seemingly seamless technological carpet of miracles, doubt persisted underneath. The cascade of comments concerning the destitution of lives through job displacement, privacy issues, and ethics raised at the advent of AI algorithms reverberated in people's daily communications as murmurs. The progress story was subtended with imperative for a mere recognition that the use of AI Integration needed to be conscious and purposeful.

• • • • • • •

Even in this exciting metropolitan energy, I found individuals — namely, someone else such as Ethan- who seemed to be an advocate of ethical AI. Our talks over the cups of coffee, however, skimmed on to the alluding aspects concerning public concerns arising from the influence of AI. It became clear that the experience of events unraveling wasn't only about the development of technology but also necessity of a human element in its path.

The workplace mimicked the greater collective discourse of society. AI tools provided us with insights that aided our decisions. The numbers indicate that using relevant data shortens search time to zero and humanizes the learning process. However, it seemed a fear of job loss concerned even my colleagues. We tackled the need for upskilling and reskilling because there was a lot of harnessing that humans and AI should work side by side, both of which demand adaptability in the workforce.

• • • • • • •

In communities outside just my professional realms, I insisted on actively promoting AI awareness through various community endeavors. These discussions, however, were not limited to algorithms and data sets analysis but opened on ethical questions concerning AI. Natural leadership was needed rather than a desire to get along with AI; through this leadership, everyone would determine the ethical standards and pattern of its use.

I revel in AI's sweet affair with humanity, an artful, merry setup that brings both fervent dreams and fearsome caution. For example, it's a history that emphasizes how we share the fate of structuralizing AI integration into wider epistemological and ontological discourses.

Our future is not pre-established by technology; it is only that which comes about as a result of our choice via the means of talking and cherished values for things that are presently undergrowth, but waste remains on hold.

· · · · · · ·

The juxtaposition of humanity and AI swirled in unforeseen ways; therefore, I find myself wanting to go further and discuss the ethical aspects of this complex relationship. It was quite clear that the ethical aspects of AI went far beyond the walls of the office.

As I was in search of comprehension, I found myself coming across cases when AI, though sophisticated, failed to cope with the complexities of human feelings. It was a strangely inverted spectacle – the machines trying to crack the code of sentiments, empathy, and moral reasoning. While I traversed this landscape, it became apparent that the inoculation of empathy into AI algorithms was not simply a technical problem but a philosophical one.

• • • • • • •

Ethan – the ethical AI advocate – was as good a companion as one could have for this journey of discovery. Our discussions even created into why morality was being ingrained into artificial intelligence. It was not just about developing machines that could replicate human behavior but by instilling them with a moral compass to guide them in the treacherous terrain of human ethics.

Our discussion chapters concern moral accountability of developers of AI, transparency in the process of algorithmic decision-making, and impossibility of biases to infiltrate the digital realm. We understood that AI had so much power, which in turn required a system of accountability and a constant conversation between the developers and users of such intelligent systems.

• • • • • • •

Within this developing story, I happened upon accounts of AI being used for good. Successful fusion of human intentions and AI was investigated in medical achievements, environmental conservation, and humanitarian aid. These cases were guiding lights, demonstrating that parallel existence of AI and human beings might result in a more perfect world.

Yet, challenges persisted. The privacy issue was loudly echoed, and the increasing reliance on AI systems spurred the argument of individual autonomy in the digital era. The balance between innovation and preserving basic human rights became an essential issue.

• • • • • • •

Like an epic saga, as I read through the chapters, it was clear that the account of AI assimilation was yet to be complete what we do today- as individuals and as a society.

The ethical issues, moral codes, as well as deliberate actions we take shall define if the romance with AI will be a lovely symphony or a noisy cacophony.

I prepare myself for the further visitation of this fast-evolving relationship, where the constants of the organic and artificial become ambiguous, and the fate of humanity and AI is a singular story. The road is far from being closed, and the discoveries that await are sure to be as riveting as they are confounding. Thus, my dear readers, let us peel away the next layers of this captivating story, where the tension between man and machine remains in play, defining the lines of our common future.

• • • • • • •

Chapter 10

Finding Balance: Navigating the Digital and Real Worlds

With screens, notifications, likes, shares, and artificial intelligence, I found myself in the house of digitalization. Yes, there was no balance between the technology and the real life.

I could say that the technology and the artificial intelligence overshadowed the richness of the real-life experience. I am grateful that I realized that there is a real world as well.

When the realization hit the mark, my journey of mindful technology use began. A journey where I am the protagonist of my own story. I ultimately learned how to dance between the digital and the real world.

I understand the world in which I am living the professional work that I do, demands the use of technology, and without the use of technology, I would rather be isolated. But when I come back home, I can do the daily chores on my own. I do not need artificial intelligence to set the lights of my room according to my mood. I do not need a robot to turn on my air-conditioner. I can do all of this on my own.

Most importantly, I realized about my background. I struggled, I worked hard to reach where I am today, and it won't be a lie—I reached here with my capabilities. I was interviewed by a dozen recruiters, and I proved them that I am skillful.

• • • • • • •

Ultimately, I understood something that lies deep in my heart— my background is important for me. It became clear that the road I walked was largely marked by challenges and sheer will. Every step contributed to where I am now. I am not exaggerating when I say my current position reflects my capabilities.

My career path made me go through many interviews with recruiters who were suspicious of my know-how and ability to fulfill the job duties. Nevertheless, I regularly proved that I was skillful despite them. Faced with several recruiters, I repeatedly demonstrated that I had the competencies they were looking for.

The bumps and obstacles in my past didn't stop me, but they were stepping stones guiding me to the self-made, capable person I am today. My conviction in myself afresh was built on the awareness that mine is a story of resilience, progress, and unfailing determination.

As I look back at the road that got me here, I appreciate that my capacities, polished through endurance, have driven me forward. The interviews, however, were not just evaluations of my skills. They were avenues for me to illustrate the resilience and ability that constitute my professional persona. Each interaction turned out to be a chance to prove that my background does not produce a minus but is a dense canvas of wise decisions, which stiffened my skills and influenced my path.

But what happens today?

Artificial intelligence is not human; there is no human at the back of the screen. The resumes are selected by artificial intelligence or maybe an algorithm. The candidates are selected via technology, the interviews are conducted virtually.

Here, please understand that I am not against virtual interviews; I am pleased that the candidates do not have to travel miles to get rejected. Now, they can give an interview sitting at the comfort of their home.

I remember commuting long hours to reach the destination on time. I used to spend money on the tickets, and at times, I skipped food because I had no money to buy a ticket for the bus for the next interview.

Getting back to the point, the selection of artificial intelligence at times skips the deserving candidates. In my case, I had no prior experience; I did not have a fancy degree; still, somehow, someone managed to see my capabilities and gave me a chance.

Here, my point is the same: A candidate may not have the relevant experience or degree, but he/she might be capable of reaching the skies.

ALL THEY WANT IS A CHANCE.

· · · · · · ·

The probability of the chance becomes zero when the artificial intelligence selects the candidate on the basis of job description and other requirements.

Please understand that I am not defending or giving priority to the ones who are not experienced. I am not putting non-experienced over experienced. But the interviews boost the morale of the candidates, or maybe they can be hired for some other position based on their skills.

• • • • • • •

I want to make clear that by experience, I mean a state where candidates can test their abilities without being forced to. Instead, I see the importance of interviews in building candidate's morale. Not only for the more experienced, interviews represent a showcase of their skills and possibilities; thus, access to roles that fall within their limits could be granted.

It is not the goal to limit the value of the experiential aspect but rather to elucidate the fact that an interview can be transformative to people at different stages of their careers. For less qualified candidates, the company provides an opportunity to show their skills, initiative, and eagerness to develop. It is also a moment for employers to disclose the dormant talent that might be scarcely found on the resume.

In addition, interviews facilitate recognition of candidates who might not fit a particular job but could bring on board valuable skills that could fit other places within the organization. The process, however, becomes a double-way road in which both parties' candidates and recruiters can find themselves mutually compatible and chart a way for collaboration.

In a nutshell, the goal is to acknowledge that though experience is important, interviews are vibrant in gauging a candidate's general fit and likely contribution. They are not only for filling up a role but for finding individuals who have the necessary skills, attitude, and adaptability to make a real contribution to the organization in several capacities.

• • • • • • •

I am grateful for my realization; I am grateful that I woke up.

A moment of reflection triggered by the buzz of my smartphone (ironic, isn't it).

Flickering through the apps became a reflex, a routine consumed by the day without conscious thought. It was at that moment I realized to redefine my relationship with technology.

Yes, I am here, not here to advocate how I cut the ties with technology and artificial intelligence.

But to advocate how I redefined my relationship with technology. To transform it from a mindless distraction to a purposeful tool.

● ● ● ● ● ● ●

Influence vs Illusion

My dear readers,

What I am sharing now is my personal approach and how I jumped on my journey of self-discovery. The first and foremost step was digital detox. I untangled myself from the constant baggage of notifications and social media feeds.

Yes, I started to become deaf to the notifications; I trained myself not to look at my notifications as a desperate and try to ignore them.

And to my wonder, I started to feel more active. I started to enjoy my cup of coffee every night.

Do you know the best thing happened to me?

I started to read again.

Yes, I was an avid reader. I used to buy piles of used books (smiles widely), and I used to read them all in the span of 2-3 days. Selling them again to them same bookstore, I used to buy more of the books.

Maybe I learned about the world through books. I learned different languages as I had a reading hobby. But, during the race of climbing up the corporate ladder and proving to the world that I am capable, I lost myself. Though I had a room full of books, people used to call it a mini library. My friends and colleagues all used to appreciate and complement my love for books, and they used to get books from my library, too.

But I never got the time to even look at it. Even though whenever I used to travel or walk through a bookstore; I used to buy books.

Sadly, I never got a chance to read them.

Getting back to the story, I got my life back after the digital noise faded. I found myself immersed in the life outside the screen. The laughter of friends and the aroma of freshly brewed coffee became the new soundtrack of my moments.

The process of mindful technology use was not at all about abandoning technology, but it was all about reclaiming control. I curated my digital space and deleted apps that were of no use. And swiped those on the front that added value to my life.

• • • • • • •

Social media transformed from a mindless scroll into a curated platform for meaningful connections and shared experiences.

I did not abandon the technology but started using it more appropriately. I mastered the power of productivity to organize my tasks more efficiently, allowing me to reclaim the moments of the real world.

All of this created a line between work and leisure, ultimately creating an integration of technology into my daily routine.

• • • • • • •

I hope my story relates with your experiences, but I will be honest; in my journey of self-discovery, I discovered the art of being present. I got myself fully immersed in the experiences that unfolded before me.

Unintentionally or intentionally, at least I learned how to strike a balance between the artificial world and the real world. Each interaction with the technology became a personal and conscious choice. Each guide by a question:

"Does this add value to my life?"

• • • • • • •

Influence vs Illusion

Despite my will or not, I have attained the art of keeping a fine balance between the artificial universe and the concrete reality that confines me. Every interaction with technology has transformed into a personal, conscious decision-making process guided by a simple yet profound question:

"Is this worth my time?"

This introspective inquiry has become my guide in traversing the constantly evolving digital domain. It compels me to evaluate every technological encounter in terms of its purpose and effect, singles out as what should concern me, the experiences that positively shape my life. It's an inner work that elicits the distinction between the artificial noise and the real content that fosters my development in real life.

In this current day of continuous connectivity, where the differentiation between the virtual and the real almost vanishes, this guiding question has been embraced as my guiding principle. I am forced to be deliberate about the decisions I make, building a conscious relationship with technology. Each click, each scroll, and each interaction are gradually passed the litmus test of value addition in accordance with that, I study, work, and live to uplift.

•••••••

In actuality, I've adopted the art of discernment in the digital age, where I understand that I possess the power to Mold my experience through my decisions. I use the question, "Does this add value to my life?" as a guardrail directing me to a genuine symbiosis of technology with my life, keeping intact the genuineness and the richness of the real world.

It was not about rejecting the digital world of the transformation; it was about reshaping my values and aspirations. It was a journey where I, the protagonist, discovered that aspect of technology where intention and awareness could enhance the beauty of real-life experiences rather than destructing them.

● ● ● ● ● ● ●

Yes, the realization hit me hard; the digital world, with its screens, notifications, and artificial intelligence, had started to overshadow the richness of my real-life world. In the era of digitalization, I realized and recognized the need for a change; it was my conscious or unconscious effort to redefine my relationship with technology. The journey of mindful technology, where I learned to strike a balance.

Despite my professional demands, I found peace in acknowledging the fact that I don't need to divert my attention every time I receive a notification. I reflected on the impact of artificial intelligence on the recruitment process and made everyone acknowledge the pros and cons.

Yes, we cannot ignore the fact that virtual interviews brought convenience; the automated selection process somehow overlooked the deserving candidates who lacked the checkboxes.

• • • • • • •

My story is not about abandoning or rejecting the technology but using it in a more mindful manner. It is an acknowledgment that technology is a tool and how to shape the experience by keeping a balance.

I went into a digital detox and trained myself to be less reactive to notifications and more present at the moment. The rediscovery of books, the joy of a cup of coffee, and the laughter of friends became the new soundtrack of my moments. Mindful technology is not about abandoning it but about reclaiming control and curating the digital space.

· · · · · · ·

Influence vs Illusion

In the area of the digital tempest, where notifications whipped up into gales and screens flickered like lightning, I set out to find peace. It was a voyage of self-examination, self-enlightenment, and a resolute exercise to find calm within the maelstrom of information and connectivity.

The first order of business was recognizing the tremendous toll digital noise was taking on my life. The constant pinging, alerting, and updating had created an ever-present dissonance that was as resounding as it was relentless. It was then that I decided to change course and make it for the soothing shores of inner peace.

The foundation of my peace journey was built on a profound awareness that I was knee-deep in digital chaos. I was emotionally drained, tired of competing against curated social media, and anxious from being tethered to technology. It turns out awareness was my first signal that there is a more peaceful way to exist.

Awareness gave me permission to disconnect intentionally. I implemented digital engagement boundaries that allowed me sacred time free from the screen tug-of-war. This wasn't a retreat from the digital world but a strategic effort to regain power over my time and attention.

• • • • • • •

My guiding principle became mindfulness. I was taught how to enjoy every moment, to live in the present without waiting for notifications now and then. Mindful living, however, went beyond screens – it helped me recognize the different textures of life and appreciate small things that matter in life, like feelings and simplicity.

The state of my mind was like a disorganized virtual space. Therefore, I moved on to cleansing the digital clutter, which meant only having what added value to my life in the digital world. This led me to delete all unwanted emails, declutter social media friends, or even arrange my files so they could look orderly, just as I felt inside myself while trying to reach inner peace.

Peace can be found both online and offline. It became a sanctuary in nature with its timeless rhythm. I would spend moments under the sky, between trees, and by moving waters. Nature's fitful dance was a poignant reminder of uncomplicated peace.

Thankfulness proved to be an influential force while pursuing peace. Each day, I tried to think about the things that made my life so rich – off- and online. Being thankful for what I have has helped me see through each day differently and remain calm about everything around me.

• • • • • • •

My journey had to involve recognizing problems and seeking assistance as well. I kept having conversations with friends, family members, and mental health practitioners, who were able to give their insights, encouragement, and some kind of shared comprehension. Thus, all our experiences in common built the support system that has continued nurturing my search for peace.

Real peace means accepting imperfection rather than striving for perfection. This meant acknowledging that there are defects and subtleties inherent in both digital world and real world as such. Accepting failure enabled me to let go of unrealistic standards that fuelled digital discontentment in me.

I found that, as I disconnected intentionally, the noise of the digital storm began to quiet. Here, my peace does not lie in technology's absence but in my conscious choices within its realm. My interaction with technology has changed; it is a journey still in progress and now fosters a peaceful coexistence between me and it, which prioritizes serenity, goals, and consciousness.

In this chapter, my wish is that these thoughts will speak to someone who recognizes that there can be silence amidst one's activities on the internet. This part should motivate you into purposeful living as well as intentional decisions so that you can take back your peace during this unique life path of yours.

· · · · · · ·

This was what happened to me in the sanctuary of my digital detox- an awesome transformation that was more of disconnecting than connecting, more of reconnecting with the true essence of life. The choice to leave the constant buzz of alerts and the light of screens was the starting point of an attentive journey into the material, the sensory, and the unmediated moments that life had to offer.

• • • • • • •

The absence of the incessant digital assault made me look for comfort in the simplicity of life's joys. The smell of pages, the haptic pleasure of turning its chapters, and the indulgent immersion in different worlds became a habit. It was somewhat a reinvention of the everlasting delight literature provides, a personal sense of relationship with the written word that surpassed the temporary nature of digital information.

Sipping a cup of coffee was suddenly elaborated into a mindful practice. Coffee is no longer a quick companion to a busy day but now a retreat to sit, appreciate, and be here. Every sip felt the heat of the mug, the fragrance of freshly brewed beans, and the orchestra of tastes that emerged in the mouth. At such moments, with the absence of digital interference, mindfulness became more than being free from digital distractions; it was about capitalizing on sensory captivity.

The laughter of friends through the stillness of this conscious separation became a valued soundtrack. The absence of a need to document each moment for consumption in the digital world enabled me to get fully absorbed in the real happiness of common activities. The subtle details of facial gestures, the rhythm of laughter, and the common bond all became the breath-taking vibrant colons of a canvas painted with the impact of human connection.

Influence vs Illusion

• • • • • • •

The mindful technology, as I found out, was not an escape from the digital world but an intentional cultivation of the virtual space. It was about regaining dominance over the intelligence that had, at some point, dictated the beat of life. The deliberate application of technological innovation, with constraints imposed by personal choice, was transformed into a resource for connecting as opposed to being an ever-present diversion.

• • • • • • •

The reintegration into the digital domain came with a newfound consciousness. Each alert was treated with perceived awareness, and social media became a space for constructive relationships rather than a browse through carefully manufactured peeks at others' lives. The digital detox was, essentially, not a retreat but a recalibration, an intentional attempt to marry technology with the values and priorities that really mattered.

This mindful voyage continues, and I realize the absolute virtue of the balance between the digital and the analog. The balance between the two realms sets up a life overflowing with experiences, connections, and a deep sense of being. The chapters that will follow let us together consider the changing relationship with technology that embraces the advantages of the digital age yet supports the preservation of the holiness of the now.

• • • • • • •

Dear Readers,

As we reach towards the end of this journey, I want to extend my heartfelt gratitude for accompanying me through the exploration of the digital world. The quest for balancing between technology and real-life experiences.

I hope my journey resonates with your experiences and prompts reflections on your relationship with technology. As we get more and more into digitalization, let's remember to ask ourselves, "Does this add value to my life?"

Thank you for being a part of this exploration. May your journey be one of intention, awareness and strike a balance between the digital and the real world.

www.ingramcontent.com/pod-product-compliance
Lightning Source LLC
LaVergne TN
LVHW051128080426
835510LV00018B/2298